MIRRAN THOUGHT

MIRRAN THOUGHT
Spitzwiesenstr. 50
90765 Fürth
Germany

www.dwmirran.de
www.empty.de
empty@empty.de

READ TWENTYTWO
(MT-624)

Print and publication by BOD
In de Tarpen 42
D-22848 Norderstedt
www.bod.de
info@bod.de

First printing 2019

MIRRAN THOUGHT is the publishing arm of
Mirran Threat, a company devoted to releasing the
music and writings of the various members of Doc
Wör Mirran. Mirran Thought and Mirran Threat are
both divisions of MT Undertainment.

Yink & Yank

Joseph B. Raimond

Written in Fürth Germany in 2017 and 2018 and Sliema, Malta 2018 .
"Untitled" and "Bill Of Rights" written together with Conny Eirich.

As always, in loving memory of Frank Abendroth and Tom Murphy.

For Conny, my perfect angel

Dedicated to Hardy Fox

Cover art by Joseph B. Raimond "Blind Twins" watercolor and ink on paper, Fürth, 2015.

This is DWM release Nr. 167

Cobblestones

It just
Aint
Anymore
What it once was
When the narrow
Misty streets promised
So many tomorrows
When the cobblestones
Still looked so foreign

Today
Only the beer
Is just as good
(maybe even better!)
Than it ever was

So,
Yes,
I'll have another
Please

Compensation

We, the midget-men
While fighting for our lives
In the gutters, the swamps
Are wasting our time
Painting bullseyes
On the groins
Of retarded presidential candidates
As their ugly sons
Wielding deadly
Iron penises
Take aim on the innocent
Before golfing at daddy's country club
And a quick rape or two
Before dinner and a scotch

The severed groins of the super-rich
Collect themselves in their
Church of choice
And demand our submission,
Our prayer for our own sacrifice
As we dine on our own innards
They conspire and plot
Huddled in their heated havens
And hatch more ugly vermin
To compensate
For their loss of genitalia

Tenses

Rapidly pushing sixty, and
Zipping along in my cool, French
Electric car

It hits me:

My dad is gone now
Tom took his own life awhile back
Frank died years ago

Jerry Garcia, Frank Zappa
John Lennon
Hundertwasser
So many of my heroes are already gone

Neil Young and Roger Waters
Are still hanging in there though

And Paul McCartney is way past
Being sixty-four

All those hippies
That used to say
Never trust anyone over thirty
Well, those that didn't vote for Trump
Have already died of old age

I think most of the music
Young people listen to
Is crap
And they call my bands dinosaurs

I am no longer considered cool

I tire easily
And have pains in my legs, back
And gut

Empty and lonely Saturday nights
No longer torture me, and
I no longer have that
Restless feeling
Or a lonely soul

My spirit wants to rest

And
Most importantly
I have finally met
The love of my life

I'm here:
I have arrived
In my future

Those Dogs

The dogs, they never back off
They're always there,
At my ankles
Biting, nipping,
Chewing on my bloody bones
Until I have to walk
On festering stumps

I try to kick them away
And I get in a good punch
Now and then
But soon enough
They're back
Back at it again
Back at devouring
What is bloody
Left of me

Mechanic

My garage mechanic
His name, by the way, is Charlie
Well,
I give him a call
When this ol' wreck
Breaks down again

He wanders over
Tightens a few bolts
Puts in a quart of oil
And gives it a good kick
Until that motor
Starts purring again

Then we shoot the shit
He tells a few tired old
Sexist jokes
Then wanders off again
To his grave
In the land of the dead
The wisest man
You'll never know

August seventeenth
One year on,
And I still don't want to go there
Fate was licking his chops,
Sharpening his knife
But I tricked him out of two more lives
And I've been feeling guilty ever since

Everyone says don't think about it
Yeah, easy for you to say
You are not one to dwell
Not one to question
Not one with such a vivid imagination

I am the one destined
To paint pictures
I am the one destined
To express such horror
With a brush and pen
I am the one who shakes in the night

Bill of Rights

If the constitution
Gives you the right
To act like an asshole
Then I have the right
To consider you one

Lock the Door

Lock the door
Don't take my stuff
My stuff is holy
I can only produce
My life saving art
If I possess it

Lock the door
Let me sleep
Don't wake me
With your hallway parties
Your grunts and groans
Your marital yelling matches
Or your middle aged sex

Fletcher Catcher

After Fletcher Catcher
Had caught Mrs. Fletcher,
It was retired, and
Sent to an early grave
With a funeral, but without ceremony

Its shallow grave desecrated,
The bones saw sunlight
For the first time in many years
As a proud father
Standing and gawking
Finally gave his starving son
A morsel of praise

Cling

I don't want
To rip it up
No, I want to cling
To each letter
Each word and phrase

Like the wood-tick
Sucking on my dog's eager blood
I want to poison you
With my existence

I want to cling to each
Valuable second
Become immortal through
My word
Whether you like it
Whether you read it
Whether you want it
Or not

Jaywalker

Jaywalking through life
I'm a rebel with a cause
Giving you only
My stiff middle finger
Because that is all
That you have ever earned

I'm gracious as fuck
And generous to boot
Because if it was up to me
You wouldn't be enjoying your freedom
To cast your votes for racism
Or to protest for hatred

At best,
You'd be in prison
Where you belong

Near

Don't go there
Don't go anywhere

Near

Those endless, warm summer days
That forgotten bench
And those evil nettles
That stung your young legs
Bowls of fresh strawberries
And a secret nip of the rum

Don't go there
Don't go anywhere

Near

That green park
A nervous, fumbling first kiss
Holding hands in the sunshine
And forgetting loneliness for just a few
Brief seconds of happiness

Don't go there
Don't go anywhere

Near

Those strange rumbling sounds
The shots, followed by the
Incessant screaming
Panic
What could have happened
What would have happened
If I had……

Mark

Clutching at each day
Grabbing for the rest
Of my allotted fifteen minutes
Banging my head against the wall
Trying to squeeze out each drop
Of, well, whatever you want to call it
Is like getting water from a stone

But, still I try

Like painting a moustache
On the Mona Lisa
Fuck you
If it doesn't fit into
Your definition of culture

Like the dirty stray dog
Pissing on the curb
I will
Leave my mark

Trying

Every time I try to open my eyes
I feel like I am blind

Every time I try to take a breath
I feel like I am suffocating

Every time I try to listen
I hear only noise

Every time I try to scream
I can only whisper

Every time I try to run
I can barely crawl

Every time I crave warmth
I start to shiver

Every time I try to feel
My heart grows cold

Every time I try to love
The hate boils over

Distance

When the sun is its furthest away
And the despair of this lonely night
Is like a noose around my waiting neck
The darkest of words race around my thoughts
Before falling into place

These darkest of hours
Create my most inspired poems

The Invisible Worm

Your invisible worm
Is slowly devouring you
Through your imaginary sins
That you should never want
That you should never lust
That you should never
Be proud of yourself

While the lowly and naïve
The poor and trusting
The dirty and wanting
Sit waiting for their worms,

The fat cats
The grunting, tie wearing
Prostitute paying
Con-men
Hiding under their plastic
Crucifixes
Jerk off on the piles of money
You were stupid enough
To send them

Droolin' Dalton

Better at shootin' his mouth
Than shootin' his load
The shitkicker bathed
In his redneck dreams
Of whisky and beer
Country music filled saloons
Gas guzzling pickups
And big-titted cowgirls

As a bud-bellied redneck
The stinkin' Trump-chumper
Drooled onto the beer-stained sofa
Of his trailer park, white trash
Domicile, turned over
And dreamed on

Culture

I'm not your damn culture
And don't even dare
To call me entertainment

Go into your museum
Of modern art
Your classical music hall
And dusty libraries
If you want to pretend
To understand your worthless culture
Put on your shallow show,
Get on your knees and
Kiss ass

And while you are busy
Doing nothing for nobody
That no one will ever care about
I am busy writing
Painting
And annoying you
With my loud music

I am my own
Culture

White Flag

Feeling the bugs
Squirming in my veins
My body shuts down
Prepared for a battle
A battle in which I would have waved
A white flag, thirty years ago

Who ever thought such a coward
Would have it in him?!?

And while,
Like all men like to do,
I was preparing for death
The fever in my tired brain
Began composing the most
Wonderful, delightful
And inspired poems

But being too sick
To get out of bed,
They were lost forever
Never to inspire anyone,
Not even me

Bring back my fever
Bring back that inspiration
Let me be an artist
Even if it means death

Football Match

The light was dimmed
But might as well have been red
For there were two whole football clubs
Camped between her legs
Unfortunately,
I was never much a football player

But the games they played!
Enough goals for a world championship
With fans cheering from the sidelines
And the beer flowing
Unfortunately,
I was never much a football player

The brainless fans go marching
For the matches between their legs
Strutting, each more manly than the next
Well-hung,
Their rulers out and ready
Fortunately,
I was never much a football player

Tug

That huge void
Is like a magnet to this
Little miniature life
Always tugging, pulling

Our insignificant souls
Always, being pulled
Nature hates a vacuum
As we go about our lives
Looking for meaning within the chaos

Our deaths, like our shadows
Always so close, clutching for us
The evil will gloat in the end
As it always does

We grow tired of pushing against
The constant tug of oblivion
Our bodies age
Grow haggard
Our minds forgetful
As we begin to lose our grip
And begin our descent

Bring On

My heart still feels so young
But the mirror
Tells me otherwise

Let the blood flow
Feel the blade as it slices
Through the leathery skin
Of this aging man
As long as it hurts
I know I am still alive

So bring on the pain
Bring on the dreams
Still unfulfilled
Bring on the carelessness
Yes, even the naiveté
Of a virgin body
And innocence
Of a young mind

But leave your regret
And mirrors
At the door

Spins

No, don't wake me just yet
Let me spin…
Turn another trick
Run another lap

Let the light of the sun
Warm my face just one more time
Between the gloom and the doom
Lies my few minutes of
Fleeting happiness

Don't bother me
While I wallow
Don't piss me off
When I'm having fun

No, don't wake me just yet
Let me spin…

Adaptable

I am the Mr.
Bendable
Pull me to a lover
Replaceable spread eagled
Don't matter whose
Names they were
Interchangeable

Or, if you prefer
Bend me to your lover
Dependable and true
Anything for you
My one and only

I am the Mr.
Bendable
The little red star presented proudly
Hiding behind my
Make America Great Again!
Slogan baseball cap
This hand can throw stones
Or, if you prefer
High-five you on the way
To the local book burning party

I am the Mr.
Bendable
Falling in love on the wet,

Cobble-stoned streets
Of a small Italian town
Or, if you prefer
Cruisin' for burgers
And pussy
On main-street USA
Don't forget the six-pack

Only the dishwasher
So deeply imbedded in my essence
Will never change

Apology

Standing on the rocky shore
Of the Malta coast
With the crashing waves
And salty air

I think about my first encounter
With this warm and happy sea
As a boy
Visiting with my nuclear family
And how disappointed I was
That there were no waves

But the sea tried to make up for it
With cool looking sea urchins
And funny fish
And with my parents still together
I was, briefly, happy

So many years, even decades later
As I so quickly approach old age
Standing on the rocky shore
Of the Malta coast
The crashing waves
And salty air
Offer their apologies
For the cruelty of nature
How she grinds all of us down
Writhers our bodies

Dements our minds
Until we are but dust
And someday,
Not even a memory

Terrier

We were all walking
Toward aunt Renate's house
Mom, dad, and my little sister
When a small terrier
Ran out of someone's garden
Ran past my mom, my dad
And my sister
And tried to bite me
On my leg

He didn't even break skin,
But that didn't stop me
From having a fear
And sometimes a loathing,
Of dogs,
For years

It has only been since I
Have been having big dogs
Live in this house with me
As part of my family
That I have slowly lost
My fear of dogs

So today,
When a dog runs up to me, mean
And menacing
I growl even louder

Back, ready to attack
And they quickly realize
I'm an even bigger, meaner bastard
Than they are
And that
I am not kidding
And today, these dogs all turn tail
And run for their lives

And although it was over forty
Years ago
I can say for sure, though
That if I ever see that fucking
Terrier again
He's gonna get a swift
Kick in the ribs!

Happy New Year!

Happy new year!
To a sad and unhappy world
That like the wicked witch
Beating on her faithful husband
Doesn't know how good she has it

Happy new year!
To a sad and unhappy world
Which only buys bad news
Wallows in its own filth
And calls it gold

Happy new year!
To a sad and unhappy world
Always on the brink of extinction
A gamble for the mighty dollar
More important
Than the lives of their
Own children

Sleep

For the homeless man
Who wakes from the
American dream
To the reality
Of the American nightmare
Of having to call a dirty sidewalk home
Disappointment lives deep
In his tired old bones

Insanity Twirl

Running from the yapping
Dogs of war and peace
Pieces of meat strip
Through the prison of my
Festering ribcage
Not letting my prisoners out
And no sunlight in

Let's go to the market
And see what measles infested flesh
We can devour in our plight
Of trying to look up the skirts
And down on the scum
Inhabited streets of our bitter youth

I am determined to fly
With or without you
Or anyone else, as you all wallow
In your rotten finger pointing
Bodies of eroding cellulite
And shit for brains
Brains

Religion

Amazing grace
Got down on her knees
And did her magic
Like god told her to do
A slurpy slimy Christian
She wants to make her god proud
Of the only talent
She really has

The old wooden pews
Stinking of all the fat asses
Torturing the wooden grain
Into a sag only matched
By the housewives' sagging tits

Gum smackin' teenage wench
Her perfume smells like
A fast food restaurant
Her boyfriend's cum
Drippin' down her skinny legs
Onto the sacred floor

As if the millions killed in the name of
Religion
Wasn't reason enough
For my stiff
Middle finger

If

If only I could believe
That all I need is love

If only I could believe
That good things come
To those who wait

If only I could believe
That I make you feel like dancing

If only I could believe
That I light up your life

If only I could believe
That you wished I was here

If only I could believe
That anyone would ever bother
To read this poem

Another Lonely Gig

With today's ration
Of his unwanted evil seed
Dripping into the filthy sink
Of his borough dwelling
The lone throbber
Went to the freezing street
To nickel and dime today's existence
To the indifferent passers-by

Smart enough to hang his
Little bo-peep diplomas
Within his four walls
But still too stupid to realize
That no one else will ever see them
Nor care

My Brothers

We pretend to be so intelligent
But we prefer to stay dumb

We claim to reach for the stars
But most of us would rather
Wallow in our own shit

We sometimes consider ourselves
Great artists
But then we are content to sit
In front of our televisions
And consume reality shows

We like to look at ourselves
As free thinkers
And we throw around words like
Freedom and liberty
But then we vote
For the tyrants and despots
Anyway

We consider ourselves
Politically correct
But then still whisper
Racists and bigoted thoughts
When we think no one
Is listening

Untitled

Sometimes,
The longest journey you
Might ever take
Is the journey
From your brain
To your heart

Most of us,
Though
Never arrive

Bang!

I remember turning ten
Thinking
"Cool! Now I'm double digit!"

And then,
In the blink of an eye
I was thirteen,
Thinking
"Cool! Now I'm a teenager!"
And my mom saying
"Oh my god,
Now I have a teenager in the house!"

And then,
In the blink of an eye
Bang!
I turned thirty
Already with a daughter
(she was still single digit then though)
And my mom saying
"Oh my god
My own son is now thirty!"

And then
In the blink of an eye
Bang!
I'm fifty-five
And me thinking

"Oh my god
My own daughter is now thirty"

Soon,
The next
Bang!
Will come,
But I won't be there to hear it
I'll be in the ground
And my daughter
Wondering who is that old woman
Staring at her from her mirror
Will be asking herself
"What was that sound?"

Matters

Sitting on the platform
A bit of time to kill
Watching trains
And
Writing poems

Which very few will ever read
And fewer still
Will ever even bother
To remember

But that doesn't matter
Because trains
And poetry
Make me happy
And now,
At this moment
That is all
That matters

Gravity & Reality

Walking down the pier
The young Italian stallion
Jumps into the motorboat
Turns on the motor
Revs it up loud a few times
For good measure
The eager tourists
May now board
For,
The champagne is chilled
The glasses twinkle
In the Italian sun

We can now all begin to pretend
That we are something
We will never be:
Rich, famous
Special

No thanks
I'll stick to my dry land
Gravity
And reality

Red Head

Thrown to the stack
Of the soon to be forgotten
Your bones, cleansed
By the flame of obscurity
Someday, no one will never know
You ever existed

Your books,
The little you read
Thrown into the heap of
Dumb propaganda and burned
(so much of what is written
is not worthy of being read even once)

Back to a little boy,
I sit here and try to write
And you constantly fill my head
With questions you wouldn't answer
And now
You can't answer

I thought I locked you away
But even in death
You constantly break out

I was never proud
Of my red hair

Loosing It

As I get older
I notice the first cracks
In this oh so perfect wall
As I begin to forget
How to spel

And its geting worse and wors
Day for day
As I feel the minuts ticking buy
The ours start stacking up
En endless towr of frustrashun
Grewin inter de sky, az my lif
Cums krumblling dern
Intu inkowherenc
Uv wurd en stile
Lunglust at der kurbsyde a live
Azi slepinter nunzenzzzzz,ölkjh,.nm
.kjnfd,.,jnöoiiu0io39ls,m.nfäÄ.....
....

Visage

I aint easy
Throwing punches into the darkness
Swinging my fists in the night
Aimlessly trying to land a punch
Into someone's complacent,
Arrogant visage

Like, trying to make a difference
Even if it is only your pain
Should be so hard

You all drive to work in the morning

A cat twitches in its sleep

My neighbor is mowing his lawn

All the while
I run in circles, going nowhere
Dumber than the dog
Chasing his tail

From Oblivion

I hate
Feeling my own heartbeat
For it shows me
Much too clearly,
Vividly
My own mortality
Always one beat away
From oblivion

I get so afraid
That that next beat
Just won't come
And I'll panic
And not know how
To jump start
This ailing heart
With time running out
And I will know
Oblivion

Nazi Anyway

I'd be happy
To knock you down
A few notches
But your intellect
Damns you to the
Basement anyway

That dumb look in your eyes
Like a beaten dog
Shows you wouldn't understand
And how could you?
You're a right wing
Piece of shit
Anyway

Like your brainless brethren
You feel safe with your few
But catch you alone
Your cowardice is only matched
By your immorality
And stupidity
Your whole life is a lie
Anyway

Watch your back
Fucker
I'm on to you

Yink & Yank

Humanity, being human
Can mean
The ugliness of greed and arrogance
The intoxication brought by too much
Power

Power
Can be merciless
Where scores of lives lost
Can be irrelevant

Irrelevance is often
Most of what I today consider
Fine art

Fine art
Should be that which touches our soul
Inspires the best in us
Gives us inspiration

Inspiration
Should lead us to music
The soundtrack
For that which makes our lives
Worth living

Living
Is something most of us
Don't know how to do anymore
As we waste
Our lives
In front of our television

Television
Once the most powerful of tools
To control the masses

The masses
As dumb as they come
Shouldn't be allowed
The vote

The vote
Abused and ignored
By the brain-dead
Middle class

The middle class
Benchmark of society
So good at looking away
Ignoring and turning off
The six o'clock
News

The news
Only sells when bad
Good news, falls by
The wayside

The Wayside
My place in this world
My place in this
Life

Life
Becomes worth living
With the smell of frying bacon
Or the sound of the midnight rain
Through your open bedroom
Window

Windows
Let us look out
Into the sunshine
But also within to
The gloom

The gloom
That dark world of despair
Always within my grasp
My only lifelong
Companion

Companion
Let us discover together the secrets
Of alcohol, sex and debauchery
Expected of us,
The poets

The poets
Yet more artists
Unemployed, creating for no one
But themselves
Trying to get published
They will kiss anyone's
Ass

Ass
A piece of it
Another benchmark
For a real man, the stud
The macho and his
Pick up

Pick up
That hot blonde at the disco
Your pencil off the floor
Your grandma from the
Train station
Or yourself, up off the floor
From among the dregs
Called humanity